Amphibian Dreams

books by A. M. Caratheodory

Amphibian Dreams

Caratheodory

Calliope Press 2007

Dedication

To Tara Brice, sculptor, designer, horsewoman
And to Craig Dillard, artist, designer, jeweler, pool-shark
And especially to Legend, Toma, Mercedes, Hank-Ra, Pan,
    Neon, Frick, Crow-Magnon, Slider, Rebel, and Yang.

Brevis esse laboro, Obscurus fio
Horace

Acknowledgments

The following poems have been published previously:
    Amaryllis (1977), *Sawtooth*.
    The Ground (1976), *Luckiamute IV*.
    Walking (1980), *Honey Creek Anthology*.
    Amphibian Dreams (1980), *Wellspring*.
    Leaves (1967), *Blue Hen Review*.
    Fossils (1982), *Four Mile Creek Review*
    Three Nights in the Heart of the Earth (1983), *Windrow*

Graphics by Rian Garcia Calusa, Tallevast, Florida
    design@riangarciacalusa.com

Copyright © 1982 2004 2007
A. M. Caratheodory
Mozart and Reason Wolf, Ltd., Wilmington, Delaware
    mozart@reasonwolf.com

Publisher's Cataloging-in-publication Data
Library of Congress Card Number: 83-1122
PS3553.A644A798 1982   811'.54

ISBN 0-911385-28-2

Second edition Second Printing
Printed in the United States of America

Contents

"because human life is itself non-progressive, and because we live and want to live so much in our isolated, insulated private life . . . great objective facts are very little experienced by us, and we find ourselves living in a strange amphibious world. ... living in many double worlds and leading many double lives ..."

Aldous Huxley, *The Human Situation*

"there is a dream dreaming us . . ."

Kalahari Bushman

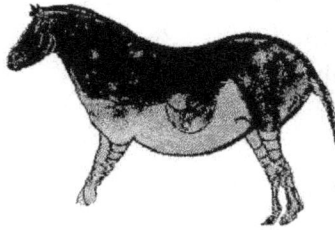

cave horse

Isolation

Lilith

We hear your voice moan over Ur,
Fatehpu and Maya,
Daughter of night.
Created simultaneously
An opposite made, but undominated,
The ideal of the dream
Too equal for Adam,
You flew from his stubbornness
To an unjust punishment.

Come from your ruined cities,
Consciousness of night,
Show us your benevolent side—
We have learned to trust our instincts, now
And will not be confounded by reason.

Release us from the single vision
Of civilization. Shatter the wall
And reconcile us with Nature,
Oh, mind of the wild,
Return the idols to the soil,
Be midwife for our rebirth
And help us return to the sensual earth.

Throw your power on the side of the low
Until wholeness is restored, open
The gates of empathy, let it mingle
With creativity. We open our hearts
To your spirit, Lilith.

Amaryllis

I saw you under moonlight and you
Reflected me. I saw you under starlight
And you grew distant and mysterious:
Your skin was the color of evening
As if you breathed that color in
And pumped the blood of sky through
Your flesh—your nipples were darker
Than your breasts—your hair a deeper
Blue—your eyes held aurora lights.

I saw you again in the forest by day
Standing under the cedars
Swaying before me in green—
Your body was a tender shoot
Nourished by the blood of leaves.
Your limbs were lighter than
Your body, as if newly grown
And your face about to bloom.

I held out my arms to you
But you turned and ran
And changed as you did:
Clay and dirt made you red and brown
Rocks on the cliff turned you grey;
You looked back once as you fell
Through air—

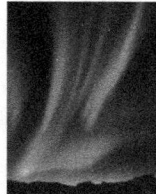

aurora australis

Ghosts in Metal

Who has been where nothing human is?
Seen the ghosts in metal
Of particles from the center,
The iridescent center of the earth,
And heard the murmurings distilled
From hard collisions; radiation
From its primordial being trapped
In matter patterns from cycles
Of stars and faintly glowing bodies?

There is history in metal
And it has meaning. Stars have history
And it lives in human memory. Faint
Pulses from the sun echo in waves
In the brain. The rhythm of the sea
Invades the copper-lead of dreams.
The battery is made and charged
Remembers ghosts in metal.

molten iron

Leaves

One leaf, then another, frees its stem
And weaves a spiral down—
The leaf we see in turning becomes invisible
And another appears. This is the operation
Of mystery: leaves turn and present us
With the strangeness of a hidden side.
They tease us—from a different
Perspective, the leaf we think we know
Turns and disappears; the new side visible
We see and name and it becomes invisible
Again. Leaves only acquire full existence
By turning.

Turning is revelation: secrets
Open. Things turn and are renewed.
The earth rotates and revolves around the sun;
The sun rotates and revolves around the galactic
Core; the galaxy rotates and revolves around
An empty center.

Which way do wolves turn, before lying
down? Which way do whirlpools turn
Or whirlwinds? The twist of oak or sycamore;
The maze of tree and lichen, or rock and moss;
The twist of a hole dug by a skunk; snakes
Coiling; the lay of cedar or balsam fronds;
Hawks wheeling, shrikes hunting; the turn
Of a shell; the helix of light or the spin
Of galaxies?

The Ground

These leaves have fallen before
With a falling that is older
Than we who watch.
And this limitless falling
We see with a vision older
Than the falling itself.

When I touch you
The coincidence of having
Touched you those countless times
With the freshness of touching you now
Dehisces my body
Into two overlapping leaves
One eternally repeating what
The other finds new for the first time
One speaking what little can be said
The other feeling what cannot
One touching the other touching
Both intertwining in spirals
About you.

To see is to see farther than the trees
Whose leaves have fallen into space before
Toward a ground that is older
Than our vision.

Kraishde forest

11

Mining Truth

We see things and know them.
We reduce expressions to words
And meanings to thoughts
And these are covered over
By the motions of living.

Feelings fade
And form a sediment of passion;
Pressure from the weight
Of feelings compresses
Memories into layers, and these
Are heated like carbon in rock
And assume a crystalline form.

Continents
Of consciousness float
On layers of dense experience.
The world is composed
Of thousands of feet of ragged memories,
Plates broken by shifting,
Floating on a molten core.

Bones outlive a creature as light outlives
A star. Heaved by inner turmoil, pieces
Penetrate the surface and invite
A deeper archaeology. The mind excavates
And elevates them to the clouds.

Crystal and bone, transformed by time,
Burn in the presence of air
And in their light is truth again.
The prism of experience splits light
To perspectives, and truth is redoubled.

Walking

The wind is warm, the stars are bright,
The sky is dark, the ground is cool;
I walk, they move, their aspects change
And pass;
They blow, they blink, they deepen,
And let the echo last.

The trees are bare, the houses dark,
For streetlight's lonely welcome home;
I listen, and catch
Them telling
Stories of their history that could
Never have existed.

The poles are lines, the lines are dim,
The weeds are bent, the road is curved;
They rise, approach, enter me,
Form a memory
And recede in the night; I walk
A way and see.

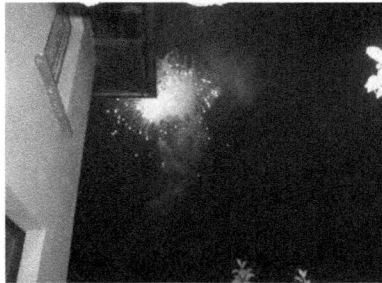

Aprilci night

Three Nights in the Heart of the Earth

Beneath the melilotus and the bee trembling
Over it, in the bright archegonium
Of ideas, the mind impregnates the object.

The seed is lost under clay and rock.
We forget the now not present, once of such
Importance. What we watch disappear
Our children will not ever know, or miss
As we did not miss what our parents forgot.
All poorer in experience.

Centuries end like nights; all things vital
Wear away, until the core is exposed.
The world slips in and out of focus
To human eyes as they age. The seed begins
To germinate, using its inheritance.
It develops in its coat: the meristem
Divides, and the leaf primordia intends.
It sends its roots to rock, where light
Dwells between grains.

Tsarina butterflies

Alone in a World of Wounds

We murder in ignorance or by accident,
A thousand ways in a thousand moments—
Every footprint leaving waste behind.

We kill for food or for convenience—
All living creatures feed on living;
Every hunger writes an autobiography
Of death. Our reverence is only
Acknowledgment of its necessity
And the fear of its consequences for us.

Our consciousness leads us from the whole;
That is how we know—in parts;
And that is its penalty. We must learn
Respect for iron, weeds, and flies
And grasp our way back.

Our obligation is to allow everything
That can to exist, not to control, promote
Or extinguish, but let each thing reach
Its full development.

Our duty is to feel, not transform or save,
To live, not evolve or finish, to respect
That the whole may feel in its diversity.

Our destiny is to turn the wheels
Of mortality and be turned under
Ourselves, that the earth may turn.

Double Lives

The Field

Weeds

The capsule drifts in the wind over ruined earth
Descends with its sphere of hairs extended.
It rests abandoned; the wind whips dust around it;
Rains drive it into a crevice.
It waits with millions of seeds from previous
Years, suspended for the right
Combination of temperature, moisture, depth,
And light.
Seizing the moment, a ragweed appears
That thrives in heat and drought.
Five thousand seeds burst from it, it perishes.
Ragweed colonizes the ground.
Then the field is a realm of ragweed, dandelion,
Lupine, foxtail, mustard, mullein, and salsify.
The earth is bound in roots; winds
Cannot scatter it or waters waste it.
Dying weeds cover it and keep it moist.

Grass

In the shade of ragweed, cheatgrass and bromus thrive
And crowd the pioneers out. The grasses bind
The earth tighter in systems of roots, like skin.

Trees

After fifteen years, a pine appears
With heavy seeds and promise of a forest.

The Lives of Weeds

A weed is an unwanted plant, invader,
cheater, destroyer, thing identified by
a derogatory name: bindweed, stinging
nettle, prickly lettuce, ragwort, puncture
vine, thistle, the enemy of all that is valuable
crowding, robbing, carrying diseases
and poisons to humans, animals, other
plants—a problem to be annihilated.

Snapdragon, fleabane, ragweed, the most
productive of plants. The seeds—dandelion,
milkweed, thistle—drift in the wind
and settle, bombs set to explode when
the ground is disturbed—thief or pioneer—
they seize their opportunities. Each seed
is a finger of life, probing to where life
is not. In extremes of heat, drought and light,
each grows and holds moisture, retards
the wind, casts a spot of shade, and finally
surrenders its substance to others. Each
changes its place a little, reproduces
and perishes and all things follow and
nothing in their basic description prepares
you to witness their ecstasy at living.

mountain weeds

The Ecstasy of Weeds

Diverse and fertile, weeds wait
Outside a profusion of possibility.
Lupine lies frozen for ten thousand years;
Thistles rest on fence rows and roadsides;
Chamomile waits to colonize vacant lots.

Our skill at gathering wild plants
And herbs is lost, and with
It the value of weeds—
Who knows that couchgrass heals?

We know nothing of them. Seeking
Leads into wildness: Bluebells,
Rose, spiral racemes.

Where shall my soul dwell?
In immortal tansy.
And where is my home?
On earth in morning glory.

The Ecstasy of Trees

Some things cannot be measured— joy
when light and water stiffen trees
and they stand.
They stand outside
of the plane of ephemeral life,
outside their own dead
flesh, outside the insubstantiality
of light.

Woman Crowded with Spirits

When her grandfather died she smiled like him,
And when her grandmother died she needed coffee
In the morning before she would smile at all.
She was melancholy as a teenager and much preferred
The company of animals. She was surrounded
By cats and, not infrequently, a deer, bluebird,
Or horse. She saved a chicken once, and a calf,
And never thereafter ate the flesh of either,
Restricting herself to asparagus and cucumber.

When her lover died she began to sing to herself
And to act dramatically on occasion.
And after her brother died she was prone to long
Walks, often making for distant streetlights
Like a moth between moons; she wrote in secret
Journals, enjoyed throwing a football,
And discovered a fascination for microscopy.
She dressed wildly and came to believe that the lives
Of others became entwined in her. Should they die
Their patterns would continue, the five hearts
Beating in parallel, impelling the five breaths
Through the shared mouth.

Then after he stopped his heart from grief predicated
On misunderstanding, she walked up the butte.
The black shape preyed silently on pine cones, tossing
Earnestly and rolling, batting them down the hill.
She kneaded her claws on the forest floor, vaguely
Aware she was once alone.

Metamorphosis

Leaves grow at angles from the stem
So that each collects the light.
Light falls slowly like the dust
That leaves collect; it is held
And its crust forms the mask we see.

The leaves are burned by day,
Their colors are stripped by layers.
The leaves are ambiguous in the wind
When the walnut tree is astonished
By a storm. Connections to the stem
Are subtle and easily overwhelmed.
Thin dry pages that once transmuted
Sun to flesh lie folded like meanings.

The leaves die and fall in winter;
Walnuts turn from green to black.
The tree stands in the cold air
With nineteen walnuts perfect and still.
A beetle in the bark digs deeper;
The center is dead, frozen cells
Surrounding nothing—a walnut turns
With a gust; the stem parts; the sphere
Turning becomes invisible and visible
Again in low sunlight. The walnut hits
The ground and splits open—there
Is no inside, only the one side folded over.

The birds of emptiness take wing.

The Cosmology of Insects

The time for gluing and spinning is done—
This the last molt by the season;
The rind suddenly bursts;
He emerges with the fresh aura of dew;
All thorns and bumps and hairs shed,
Now bare and white and smooth;
Eyes darken first, then the body turns brown
And colors form; eyes shimmer
With hues of blue and gold in a perfect
Geometry of sight;
Spots of light combine into a mosaic;
The image of the branch is clear and sharp,
Yellow against the violet sky.
Antennae wave to evaluate shapes surrounding,
Odors of food and enemies and others.
Wings—clear membranes of delicate glass
Stiffen with air and blood—tremor;
The body pulsates, waves move into the wings,
Which beat with force, and he is hurled
Into the air, violently, out of control.
The day: light moves slowly, its pressure
Pushes down; the sound of light winds
Through hollow needles.
The eyes never close, the gullet never fills;
Facing upwind for the scent and promise
Of completion in light—ephemeral light.

ladybird beetles

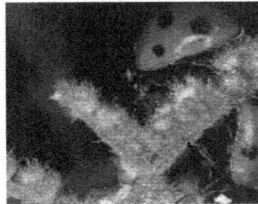

Kepler's Beast

The parts lack visible connection, but a minnow
Recognizes another minnow, and birds hear other
Birds as each marks out a territory. Birds inform
The fish of the Pacific about the state
Of vegetation in the Cascades. Each living
Being has its own sphere and these overlap
Around the earth. The bark of a coyote or twitter
Of a sparrow contribute to the whole. The earth
Is a great round beast.

Amphibian Dreams

The arc has been described,
The victim seized.
The tongue recoils, ingesting fly.
The waters smooth and the shiny
Body settles again.
Silence returns to the pond.

His sight a Pythagorean quest
For the meaning of curves;
The eyes transparent, his body
Sinks in the cool murk,
Lord of two mediums.
In formless water, he dreams
Of the sharpness of air.

frog

The Metaphysics of Order

The candles of the pines have all turned down
In the cold; the evening torrents
Through the needles, and a porcupine
Chews the tender bark.

The dead fir shoulders the sky, bones
Extended—a woodpecker thrills
The air with her ax. As the sun moves,
Shadows move and reveal the tree
Has no front or back.

Cattails line the edge of the pond;
The earth vibrates as it turns
And the surface trembles. The movement
Of air circulates with the memory of all
The revolutions of the earth. The fish
Are still in their constant water.

The droppings of a bear point up the hill
But no bear is seen.
Gophers make honeycombs in dirt. Coyotes
Bark and burrow to the roots of heat.
A deer is surprised leaving the field
Where winter wheat suffer the delirium
Of weeds. The last geese pass; some absent.

White hills invade brown, snow settles
On the meniscus in the pail disguising
The waste of life. The field stretches and curves,
Folded and folded over, drifting with motion.
Crystal white hills frame a small white sun,
Glowing faintly on the horizon, packed

With crystal lattices—the field folded around
It. Memory complicates light around the star
And hills and draws them into another whole,
Smaller and dreamlike.

Devotee of Storms

You don't know me and I don't care
I call storms when I can and when
I can't, I revel in their power. I can
be beaten
Flat and rise before the next front,
The wildness of wind and water
reflected in my demeanor.
And when light flashes
Between the clouds something
flashes between us until the balance
is restored and we're quiet, but
I don't know you and you can't share
your way with flowers or where
you go. Winds whirl and remove
The furniture of existence
from our presence
Until we are both alone
in our places.

Cloud

Once human, now dispersed
above the earth, particles suspended
together in constant motion—
but from your distance I look solid
and whole. Then slight temperature
and pressure changes let me precipitate
down, gathering lamina. As I drop
through layers, impurities
condense, growing
            I fall
enter into bodies, cool machines, collect
in streams and pools, know them well
and depart, evaporate with the wind. Rise
out of touch and move in shapes
of fantasy. Although I am bound
to the surface of the earth
by gravity, and though I must touch
you to live, It is the rising and
                    falling
I love.

Botev afternoon

Signs

I.
A log had been destroyed—torn apart by claws—
Scat with prune pits surrounded the prune tree.
One afternoon a shadow—fifty-gallon-barrel
bear-size—crossed the edge of the field.
This morning, an apple tree was shredded.

II.
A tribe of deer stare at my trailer
lit up on a moonless night.
One challenges me: Are you whole?
Can you be this complacent in the snow?

I stare at them on the edge of the circle
until a frog croaks underneath the floor.
They are gone.

III.
The mountain bluebirds came back
one last time in November
to check the fencepost
for next year.

No one noticed them pass
the store or saw them
from the highway so
invisibly they fly.

cave deer

Sea Anemone and Crab

> I was at home
> And should have been most happy—but I saw
> Too far into the sea, where every maw
> The greater on the less feeds evermore.
>
> Keats

I had thought all beasts alone, against
The world—but chimpanzees cry warnings
To antelope; satisfied wolves walk among elk,
Where all elk allowed a part to nourish
The wolf stomach that takes a share
From microbes within, to sustain blood
At whose centers live strange beings,
That can burn without burning.

The invader is conquered and tamed
Until the two live in dependency,
Two beings making three in a community
Of one—no one lives alone. Lichen
Break rock. Bacteria live at the roots
Of peas, and peas can dissolve iron
And build prairies.

The hermit crab claims a shell
To which a sea anemone attaches,
Protecting the crab with poison nettles
And feeding on the bits of leftovers.
When the crab moves, he takes his plants.

All nourishes all in a cycle
Of renewal—incomprehensible.
Destruction feeds the ecstasy of creation—

27

The Way of the Deer

There is a way of knowing
That is the way of the deer.
You will realize you know it
That you are already like
And unlike the deer
In feeling and thought.

The deer embodies experience;
The vitality and wisdom of
Her body ruins complete rationality
And loosens up our categories—
No monster Pan,
But a small being
Pleased at fitting between
The woods and fields so well.

How can you browse grass or rub
A tree without becoming it?
Dizzy with eating, exposed,
She scratches the surface
Of wholeness with her hooves,
With her green eyes.

cave deer

Wolf

I am wolf. I chase the deer who chase the grass
who chase the sun. Grass is light, deer is light, wolf
is light, all is light. Across asia, siberia, america, europe,
I chase deer and mice and light. Not alone, no, always
with a family, always at home.

        I was raised by my parents,
uncles, aunts, brothers, sisters, and friends. I learned
cycles of heat, the meanings of clouds, the scent of prey,
the feel of grass—the culture of our ways: how to play,
and hunt and play. I found a mate, we played, shared
mice and moon and fluid—our way of mating is beyond
you—we lock and turn and we hold and hold until
we are dry and fall apart. We made a den; cubs came
from us and we joyed in their presence, teaching them
how to play, how to find food and eat, play and sleep
and play and play.

        We were many, a populous people,
until your kind came with sharper teeth, faster claws,
greater numbers—many, many more—and took
our homes, our places, our food. There were fewer
places, fewer pups, fewer of us, then almost none—
and light has lost so many of its facets.

        I am wolf.
I am old and stiff. I need to piss—
ah howl with me one more time for the missing
and the unborn, for lost worlds and lost light—
now howl!

    (chorus)

Wolf News

This is what I, wolf, see: tracks, lines, bent
stalks, small prints in dirt—but there
are primary trails: vapors, clouds of smell,
the history of all who passed before me, their mood
and direction, health and intent, messages
that cannot go unread, only evaporate and be replaced
by newer ones, layer upon layer of deep rich
sediment, exhalations, urinations, oils, saliva,
hairs, excretions, the signs that let me taste who
ranks, who rejects, who mates, or not, who travels,
who kills, who sickens, who is at home, who is not,
whatever is dropped, brushed, torn, left behind,
whatever can be carried by wind and air and can tell
me the story of the hour, whatever I can use
to complete my own needs and understanding,
though there are things I do not know—
how do butterflies die? Do they just land, fold
their wings and wait, not to fly again? Does time
slow, or being extend? My own death
may not be as easy, but you can taste
that story later.

Legend wolf

Convolutions

How the levels of salt and water have changed;
  Which streams lead to winter plankton;
    What canyons too deep, what volcanoes to avoid;
    Where the floating shadows came to destroy;
And where the temperatures rise and food is scarce;
  Where cascading rivulets excite flippers
    And tumble the body until the cold
      Awakens the need to surface.

Songs, songs for saving thoughts of wiser,
  Farther-traveled individuals or tasting
    Great adventures—history of thought in sound—
    Beauty of speaking them again. Songs
For entertaining, for mating—giving
  Of sperm and air, for expressing the intricacy
    Of balance, for creating fluid ideas
      That crest and evaporate in spume.

The invention of stories to explain the working
  Of waves and the purpose of breathing,
    Indeterminacy of water, the strangeness of air
And its relation to death, the substance
    Of other intelligent beings—the role
Of reason to mold the universe and increase it.

cave tunny

Dreaming

Masks

Bear masks, elk masks traced
On the wall of the cave.
We put on their skins and faces
To learn how they behaved.
They were kin and we needed them
As they needed wolves and men.
We took only the weakest,
The sick and old. Their strength
Was ours, we would not let
It ever diminish or grow cold.

Now the elk are silent, photographs
Show only hide and not the motive.
The real face is never seen. And men
Kill the strongest for trophies
And dismiss our art. The image
Of the elk is seen on mettal cans
In the stream—The image
of the bear on boot polish.

We saw strangeness and sanctity
Not the human stink on every feature.
The bear was our father, elk helped
Us to be human. We changed
Ourselves to fit the earth. We fit
Ourselves to please the earth.
You will share our fate—faster
Now in ignorance' full light.

sorcerer

Fossils

I asked for directions in Stillwater
The quarry wasn't hard to find. I
could see the whole Mississippi valley
When most of equatorial America
Was covered in Carboniferous water
Flooded and reflooded until continents
Were welded together in Pangaea
Building mountains over the Tethys sea
Glaciation, extinction—all close to me.

I clambered down and reached a fossil—
A broken core of stem from a giant
Horsetail, fluted like a column of Pompeii.
I put it aside and explored the floor
A piece of fossilized burrow—a worm
Wove an inward spiral that far outlived
The worm—and there—a treasure!
I hammered the pale limestone—the
Outline of a dragonfly opened, half
A meter wide, how delicate, amazing
That so few are saved.

Plants take carbon from the air; animals
Take plants and die themselves; carbon
In reused and deposited in earth. After
Death, this, this emperor of the air
Was covered by sediment, his substance
Leached by water, minerals and silica
Filling cell walls, until only traces
Of life were left, sleeping in time.

Drops surprised me—I hadn't thought
Of rain—Dinantian limestone formed
In shallow seas, then, later, Silesian mudstone

Contained its measure of coal—suddenly
I was wet—my hand hummed with life—
I dropped the fossil, stepped back, then
Forward. It wasn't a fossil, it was alive,
No, it was a fossil, it couldn't live
And subvert the intent of time.
As the stone dissolved from it,
The dragonfly shot to a few meters away,
Hovering, in life-giving rain.
I searched for the others dropped—
There were moving tracks in a puddle
As a worm filtered particles from the water—
A scaly trunk rose from the mud to twice
No, ten or more, times my height, forking
At the top with tufts of leaves,
Strange, long, single leaves—a club
Moss, extinct. Other things began to move,
Other sounds, the whole quarry buzzing—
Oh, God, the end? a dream?

Strange forms grew up around me in the rain
To hissings, croaks and splashes; movements
In air, earth and water. These were not
The rings of water's light, these were joys
And surprises at finding life, the chaos
Of desire for feeling and speaking. I watched
As the rain gave birth to a whole Westphalian
Forest. As the water covered my knees,
I stepped to a hummock. The rain sought
Its level on the face of earth. Open
Canopies of club mosses framed marshy pools,
Giant horsetails with simple leaves
In circlets, tree ferns with elaborate,
Feathery fans, tall, slender trees with crowns
Of branches and cones—a mayfly carried
Yellow pollen to fertile seeds—green

Creepers with wedge-shaped leaves. The dragonfly
Was gone, but I saw flies, cockroaches, spiders,
Centipedes—a flash of red, salamander?
I could not move, the rain had leached my will.
I stood as the forest aged and fell, as water
Covered us all; weeds floated past my face.
The coal forests flooded; trees and animals fell
Into mudstone—only mussels and lampshells
Moved. I waited. A lone trilobite in its armored
Shell crawled by, feeding obliviously; light
Reflected off a faceted eye before it scooped
A resting place in mud. Shark tore a fish
With heavy plates and heavy jaws, then ate
The pieces. I tried to hold my breath, but
I wasn't breathing. A rare fish feeding on algae.
Corals build up. Crayfish hurry on secret
Errands. I saw a conical shell with rings,
A nautilus, ammonites, sea lilies, radiolaria,
A new community form.

It lived and died. Silt rained. The continent
Lifted and Namurian seas departed, before
The horizon of reptiles. Mountains rose
From unimaginable collisions. Volcanic ash;
The sun. Then it rained again. How many times
The seas came and went I cannot tell. Life
Surrounded me always, though individuals fell
And groups became extinct. Three hundred million
Years passed in minutes. The sun became
A shuttered arc, a line, across the sky.

Clouds passed over, water dripped from an oak
Leaf and trickled through the quarried rock—
I have only just arrived . . .

The Cave of Night

She lay on her side,
Indifferent in sleep
Slowly music, and light
Dancers around a fire
One held up a metal disk
.

She woke, gazing at the wall
Its smoothness dissolved
As from acid on a copper
Sesterce—Vespacian's profile
She blinked
Redimensioned.
The smoothness was scored with scratches
As she watched
Scratches outlined figures sharply
Across a fissure
Altamira, the code of mystery
Renewed in red.
The deer are running.

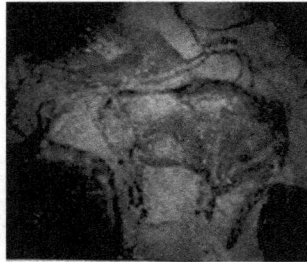

cave bull

Horses Under Lightning

All afternoon warm humid air rose above
the hill overlooking Potlatch, Idaho.
The horses were pastured in the orchard
in the portable electric corral by the house.

I brushed insect eggs from the black hair
on Roma's chest. You doctored the cut
on Figurina's leg; we both had to push
Ballerina's nose from our work. You said
she has to be trained soon. She wickered
agreement and we laughed. The dark bay
looked just like her mother. Then we talked
on the porch as the sun set to the sounds
of horses grazing. Roma stood guard
against every shadow or unexplained
motion. The air was still unstable, waiting
to be overturned. Unseen in the forming
cloud the collision of moving particles
redistributed charges.

We went to bed as the cloud built over
us and slept until violent booms woke us.
The cloud had reached maturity, smashing
air, rattling the windows with hard rain.
The horses screamed.

With a dead flashlight and an empty lantern
we went outside to calm the horses.
The rain soaked us instantly, one gasp
and it was already too late to go back
inside. The absolute dark forced us to stop
and wait less than three feet from the house.

We had to wait for each flash for a tenth
of a second of light before moving a step
closer, after which the darkness deepened
even more. I took Roma, you the mother
and daughter. I did not want to be here,
but the barn was half a mile away. We had
to keep them from running. Roma
was wild and rearing, each movement became
a still picture illuminated by a stroke of light;
I reached her on the fourth try. I stroked
her neck and withers slowly with one hand
keeping the other on her chest to track her.
I whispered soothingly into her nose—a bolt
showed white starred face and frightened eyes.

It was like being on the floor of the factory
of creation where electric power—ten
thousand amps, a hundred million volts,
per bolt—surged between the generators.
Charges built between the negative cloud
and its positive shadow on the earth until
they exceeded the insulation of air. The current
flowed in a path and the return stroke flared
with the heat of the sun. The path and stroke
hit too fast to tell apart. A crack and instantly
a bang as air exploded. My teeth hurt
my ears hurt. I saw the sound bounce off
every thing—I saw the waves vibrate air
and trunks of trees. I watched as a tall cedar
down the slope—my favorite for sitting under—
was struck—twenty foot shards were rammed
into the ground around the trunk, an instant
perfect wooden cone—a small flame flickered
at the ruined vertex, then went out.

Another strike destroyed the southwest corner
fencepost, you said. I saw you now and then
made still by a flash. I felt myself absorbing
energy somehow or maybe just vibrating
in sympathy. The horses were wild. The night,
the light, was wild. I saw it through them.

After an hour the lightning moved northeast,
rumbling as different parts of the cloud reported
their progress, or differences with the ground,
or unhappiness with the attitude of another,
light flashing between them. The air
had turned and balance was restored.
All things recharged. The rain became
steady. The horses were calm and hung
their heads in the rain. We stood beside
them, looking up. I did not want to move.

We went back inside, left clothing soaked
on the porch. Every night since is pallid
and dull, except sometimes when I look
in your eyes or Roma's and see the ghosts
of lightning.

cave horse

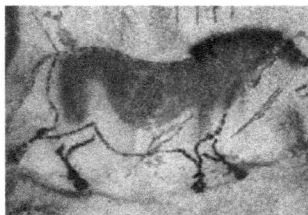

Three Perspectives from an Irish Forest

September

In the Cork countryside, I walked outside the woods,
looking into the shadows for the source of movement.
I saw none but went in. I waited by an oak. alone,
separate, waited longer until the shadows covered me.

Someone courted us by walking around and pausing,
coming inside; but he went no further and we could
not move to him. We waited beside him and he waited
beside us, until the ground and shadows connected us.

I saw him walking, then go into the cove and as he
reached into the trees, his arms lengthened
and the roots came up and branches lowered until
I could not tell where trees began and he disappeared.

Altazor Forest

40

Three Perspectives from an Irish Forest

February

I saw her lying beneath an alder, in brown lace;
I went to her and lay down and touched her face.
Her brown hair hung over me and through its veil
I met her eyes and felt her fingernails on my side.

He appeared, as I was lying with a beam of sun,
his handsome skin, like my fur, shining with health
and need. He lay beside me and offered his life
which I took in my need and made a part of mine.

I watched a man walk directly through the forest
to where a bear lay in the ambient light by her den.
He lay directly down and touched her muzzle; saliva
rolled from her mouth to his, running down his cheek,
as she tore him open with her claws and feasted.

bear den view

Three Perspectives from an Irish Forest

November

I was sitting under the alder, admiring the many
mushrooms—my hands reached into the soil
and brought up masses of threads—fungus roots,
the symbiotic net that holds the forest together,
orange, white, gold—I tasted a few. Tired, I lay
down on the spongy forest bed. When I awoke
I felt refreshed, more alert and complete.

She was here, we touched, then my filaments
blended with her flesh, probed her cortex cells,
and what she was missing and what I was missing
balanced. I enhanced her ability to draw elements
from the soil, air and water and she gave me new
elements, a wonderful new mobility, and a way
to speak to the moving others—the eaters.

The forester was sitting under the tree examining
something. She rubbed it, sniffed it, tasted it, smiled
and lay down—colored threads swelled over her
suddenly then receded back into the earth. I paused,
confused by what I had seen. Then she arose, turned
like someone blind, until her eyes focused on me,
golden orange highlights flashed in her irises.

(The roots of many trees create a symbiotic relationship with an
orange-colored sponge-like fungus called mycorrhiza. The tree
roots provide sustenance to the fungus, which absorbs nitrogen
and minerals that the tree uses. The fungal hyphae decompose
organic matter and cycle the nutrients directly to the host root,
allowing trees to chemically share nutrients and information.)

Three Perspectives from an Irish Forest

April

I sat on a rock, cool to the touch, not welcoming.
I saw all the past change from that perspective,
what it was like to grow by accretion that cannot
be measured with heartbeats, what it is like
to be broken by ice and lichens. My bones.

A moment of consciousness but a thousand years
have passed, and the sum of all my consciousness
is the image of forests moving like shadows across
land—and this idea, that moving from a molten
past floating dream to a solid gives me voice.

She was just a hiker who lay on a rock in the sun
stretched her arms and molded her back to
the curve. She was so still I took her for dead
and grey as the rock underneath. Then the fingers
spread, and the deep thrumming began ...

hiker

Three Perspectives from an Irish Forest

June

I lay down in a grassy depression. The lines
I thought were roots were bones, as white
as eyes, joined by a thought that the spirit might
match with mine, might offer a wild
pulse to my heart and link another mind.

The bones rose up and held him lightly, as if
they were mere fingers of light. The form spoke
of its life as a wolf of the wood, how it lived and died,
how it lay down one last time on the pine needles
and let the life exhale. I heard the sigh, the words.

My spirit found a home, another hunter
as clever and loyal, another expression
of the impulse to breathe, to prowl,
to taste of life, the chance to howl
for every storm, and run and dance.

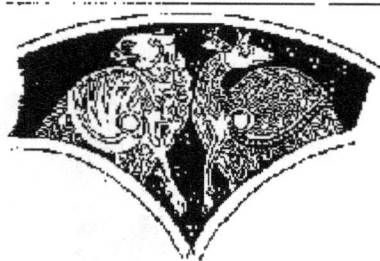

mythical beasts

In the Vanished Forest

At a meeting in Ireland. I overhear a woman talking
about magic. She is dark, her name is Katherine.

That night I buy ice cream for dinner. On my way
to the camp ground, I meet Anne and others. We
talk. There are few old people like me. Not many
males, like me. I go to sleep on an earthen mound
in the park. Cold, no blankets. Strange dreams.

The next day more talk of magic. Katherine asks
me if I can do magic. I say yes, of sorts. She says, for
example? I shrug and say a few simple things.

That afternoon, we are walking in the woods outside
Blarney. There are poles on the ground, cut a while
ago. I find a few nails, some blocks and make a small
set of stilts. One of the boys tries it and walks. I say
that is magic! The witches seem peeved. They ask for
better magic. I think about rain.

Then a young deer walks out of the woods onto
the trail near me. I stay still. The deer walks by me,
stops and touches my hand with her nose. I look
at the witches, then down at the deer's front hooves.
They are multicolored paisley almost as if painted. I
point out the hooves to the witches. The deer leaps
the fence back into the woods.

We walk on. The witches ask me if I can call animals.
I say no, only thunder. They ask if I will. I say no.
Exasperated, I hold my arms out from my side. Sud-
denly a snowy owl lands on the wire fence opposite
me and sits with both wings outspread. I look; she

looks; everyone looks. She drops off the fence
on the other side to the ground. I think she may fly away.
I put one arm to my side and the other hand
on my shoulder. The owl flies to my shoulder. I move my
hand to cover my head so she will not strike
it. She taps my fingernails with her beak. I crouch down.
The owl drops to the ground. I stroke
the owl's head and back. The younger girls and boys
come closer. I ask them if they would like to touch
the owl. They say yes, and several do tentatively. I notice
the owls claws are painted different colors.

The owl flies back to my shoulder; she seems heavier
and larger. I ask her if she is a gypsy.

                              She says, "who?"
I say I cannot begin to guess her name nor would I dare
assign one.

             She says, "then you cannot know me."
She now has spangles; her legs are longer—resembles
more a little girl dressed as an owl. She has dark cloth
with silver threads around her waist. We talk magic.

Suddenly it is dawn. She is standing beside me, about
four feet tall now. I ask her if she must go.

                                 She says
it would be best. I help her to my shoulders to fly
into the woods.

               She leaps and glides but lands face down
in the grass—she is more girl than owl.

                                I run
to her side and help her up. She blows air over her feath-
ers in exasperation.

                 Too long, she says. I kiss her,
but her lips are already hard. She is smaller.

I lift her and launch her into the woods. As she glides
away from me she seems to shrink. She lands
on a low tree limb, glances back, her neck twisting
all the way around.
　　　　　　　She flies up to a larger branch,
perhaps confused by the light or uncomfortable.
Then she glides through the trees towards the dark
forest, becoming smaller until she is gone.

I look for feathers; there are none. I look at the sky;
it is overcast. Everyone has left.
　　　　　　　　No one even noticed
my recreated beech forest—
　　　　　　　vanished 2000 years ago.

beech forest

Soul Haiku

Errors and dreams are
the sources of creation
and my life fuels them.

Without the scrawking
jays or knotted roots your sacred
touch is not enough.

Daphne from laurel
your body bends towards me
reversing the chase.

Peel an onion by
layers—at the center of
unity—nothing.

On a trail through woods
a spider clings to my arm—
stickiness of life.

Waiting on meters
the wrens are patient for bugs
smashed on car bumpers.

Sitting on the tip
of the pine, the cardinal
hinges it to sky.

Playing on the bole
of an oak, squirrel spirals
downward—shadow tail.

Thorned thistle, tender,
pushes its way through concrete—
always rock-breaker.

Struck by hot lightning
the oak raises its bare limbs
in astonishment.

buzzard

Knowing Why

I've learned a few things (not that many, though).
I know why the leaves fall in October and I know
why the gopher snake bites when you pick him up.
I know why water runs downhill and where it goes
and I know why an owl flies and the lichen grows.

> The leaves fall because the maple protects
> itself from the dark and cold, and a snake bites
> because he doesn't know you or your intention.
> Water seeks a resting place, a stable situation,
> and the owl has to catch her food, and lichens
> are trying to split every barren rock open.

But don't ask me why you left me—did you need
to protect yourself? Did you not know me? Did
you need a place to rest where I would not pester
you? Were you hungry or did you just need to
degrade me? I don't know. I really don't know why.

> But, I do know that now I am more at home
> with snakes and owls, squirrels and lizards
> than I ever will be with your ambitious
> neglect. I know why a coyote howls, but not
> why I must learn to. I know why a lion hunts
> and rests alone, but not why I continue to.

I don't know why some swans don't mate for life
while others do. I don't know why some wolves
never mate and others do. I know why I want you
for life, but I don't know what you want—
I don't know and I know you can't tell me—
and I worry that it's too late, but I don't know why.

Just a Smile

When God made me he put essences of other beings
into me: A piece of wolf, a bit of crow, a few needles
from a pine tree, a spot of fungus, some worm,
chunks of rock, a little beetle wing, whatever else
was lying around. Then, I enjoyed being with all
my relatives, and I was at home wherever I was.
But then I loved you and you made me more
human, so much so that I neglected the other
connections—almost forgot them. We kept
to the concrete city and exclusively human
things. We celebrated human differences
and human heights, but then you left me
for a simple human being—you told me to go.

So now I live with real people—owls and lizards,
grasses, coyotes, lichen—without you. I remember
them and yet I have not forgotten you or the time
I was almost dead. I run quietly through the night;
I am ruthless. I lick the blood. I sit and fumble
through the soil, empty and full, shredding bark
and twigs, tasting the not-quite-sweet cambium.
I open under the sun, extending tendrils down
between roots, between diatoms and water
drops. At last my shredded spirit is diffuse; maybe
it will never return, but maybe it will never need to.

Now the city has crushed you and you need me
and I have come to help you, but when I show
my teeth, are you sure it's just a smile? When
I caress your head, when I explore your fingers,
is it because you were my mate or just my prey?

Forest Passage

I don't tell anyone where I am, just
like I didn't tell anyone there where
I was going. Now, I'm in the forest, but
I'm not alone, no, everyone here has heard
me stumble through the brush and vines,
but they let me go my own way. The painted
turtle couldn't escape and had to be held,
as unwilling as you but easier to catch. He
showed me the direction to the stream.
The bull snake path pulled my gaze to
the berries that were old but very sweet.
I poked into the old dry leaves that crinkled
with his passage—never did see him.

Fir trees protect me from the sun;
a breeze winds around me exhausted
from forcing its way past the edge
trees' low boughs, but welcome and scented.
A chipmunk scrambles out of reach
along a log, certain that I'm hungry
for her—and only her flesh.
Across the sky, the eidolons flirt
before turning into merely clouds
that whirl into other shapes.
Birds sing and let me know when
someone's coming so I can hide as well.
Turkey buzzards patrol the whole
forest just above the treetops.

I'm not upset, I'm not afraid, the harm
that's possible is not the cruel kind.
Bear rambles along, leaving berry-rich
piles of dung; I poke it with a stick
to see if it's still warm. It is.

Now it's dark, I walk through the trees
just slightly darker than the deer
trail slightly darker than the sky beyond.
A mountain lion watches without giving
away her position—I know because I smell
her slightly stronger than the leaves.

Every passing moment something human
slips away from me like night fog.
I am incapable of feeling, although
I can move quietly like a lion
through the needle-dry trees.
I am as cool as the moss that grows
over old logs. I am as dark
as the soil under decayed wood.
I am as content as the black bear with
the richness of fall berries. Every day I close
myself a little more to useless information.
Soon I will be incapable of speech.

panther

Tough Questions

When men ask me how I lived,
what I did, with what success,
I don't know what to say.
When deer ask me how I lived,
I just relate my favorite apples
after the first frost. When coyotes ask me
what I did, I yield and relive our chases
through a sun-dried field. When you
ask me what I am, I just smile.
I have no proof, one memory is enough.

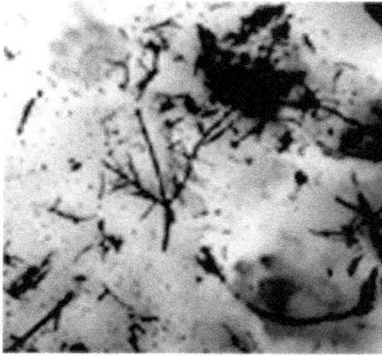

marten tracks

A. M. Caratheodory was born at the time of the largest solar eruption ever recorded—a fact he discovered when he became interested in astronomy. After basic schooling Virginia, he attended the University at Charlottesville, where he studied astrophysics. His work on mathematical models of stars received awards from NSF, NASA, USN, USAF, Bausch & Lomb, among others.

Dropping out of school as a conscientious objector and peace activist, he was drafted. He enlisted in the Air Force, working as a microwave researcher, satellite track technician, and janitor. After an honorary discharge, he worked as an observer, research assistant, then research associate in astrophysics for a number of installations, including the MIT Cambridge Research Labs, Lunar and Planetary Lab, and Arizona's Steward Observatory.

After three federal budget cuts suggested a change in careers, he worked at a series of jobs that included artist's model, lifeguard, truck driver, dishwasher, gardener, bookstore clerk, library supervisor, gymnastics teacher, printer, book editor, opera set painter, animal hospital attendant, television repair-man, auto mechanic apprentice, and systems engineer.

Returning to school, he took courses in psychology, biology, and ecology. As a teaching assistant, he developed and taught courses in ecology and ecological ethics. On various research grants, he studied wolves in Alaska, Norway, Siberia, and Bulgaria. Since then, he started his own business in ecological design, with contracts in three states.

Finding that his experience followed Auden's prescription for poets, he has written in poetic, as well as scientific, forms. He has been published in numerous regional journals; since 1984, he has worked only on book-length themes. He continues to work hard to keep to the dictates of Wordsworth and Novalis to be a good poet.

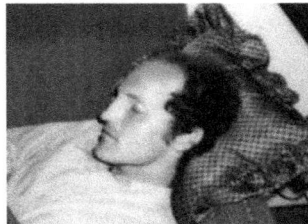

working

Colophon
Book Design: A. M. Caratheodory
Cover graphic: Ulrike de Chardin
Graphics: Rian Garcia Calusa
Cave Paintings: Web sources
Photographs (Altazor): Cam Woulfe
Display text: Adobe Caslon Pro
Body text: Adobe Caslon Pro
Formatting: Indesign
Hardware: Mac G5

home

www.ingramcontent.com/pod-product-compliance
Lightning Source LLC
Chambersburg PA
CBHW020523030426
42337CB00011B/528